Acknowledgements

P9-DJA-859

To my Mom and Dad
Charlene Lasley and the late Joe Lasley
for always believing in me.

To my network marketing family,
corporate and field,
for their inspiration and encouragement.

To my husband Robert
and my children Joni and Cody
for their patience, understanding, and support.

Thank you for allowing me to fulfill this dream.

WHATEVER IT TAKES!

The AWESOME POWER of SPOUSAL SUPPORT in NETWORK MARKETING

My Story by DONNA FASON

Whatever It Takes!
by Donna Fason
Published by Whatever It Takes, Inc.
dba: WIT Publishing
4844 Hwy 36 West
Searcy, AR 72143
donnafason@aol.com
Phone: 501-514-3103

First Printing: May 2007
Second Printing: July 2014
Printed in the United States of America

ISBN: 978-0-692-23547-8

CONTENTS

WHATEVER
IT TAKES
PLATINUM
WEEKEND
JUNE 2003

Foreword

by Chris Widener

There have been three times in my adult life when I have made major changes in my life. The first was in 1988 when I packed up my 1974 Camaro and moved from my hometown of Seattle to northern New Jersey to begin my first job after college. The second was three years later when I packed up again and moved back to Seattle to launch out on my own. The last was in 2002 when I went from being a part-time speaker and author to being a full-time speaker and author.

In each situation, the support of my wife Lisa was—and this is an understatement—invaluable. The importance of what Donna Fason writes about in *Whatever It Takes* cannot be drilled in deep enough: The support of a spouse in network marketing, or any endeavor for that matter, is undeniably key to an individual's success. While Donna writes from the wife's perspective, the opposite is also true. A husband's loving and positive support for his wife and her pursuits is equally important. The relationship with a spouse is the single most important relationship married people have on earth, and the health of it will dictate to a great degree how successful we become in this life.

A spouse can make or break us in our work. If they give us their unconditional love and support, they can become the proverbial "wind in our sails." If they are negative and unsupportive, they can take the very life out of us. Even if we do achieve financial success in our business, having an unsupportive spouse takes most of the joy out of it. Ultimately, what we strive for is total success: financial and business success with a happy marriage and family life as well.

Donna is right on track with her guidance here.

First of all, she has lived the spectrum of financial situations. She and Robert know what it means to be broke and struggling. This is not a book of pie-in-the-sky platitudes. No one can say, "Well, it is easy to be supportive when you have *your* kind of success." No, Robert and Donna have the success they do *because* of their attitudes and positive outlook. Donna's attitude change and support played a major role in their family's success and the message here is simple: You can do the same!

Some key points for you as you read the book:

- Network marketing is a viable business that can be embraced and enjoyed. Donna shows how she had to overcome her negative attitude about the business itself. Millions of people are involved in network marketing and direct sales and do quite well for themselves. They enjoy the freedom that comes from owning their own lucrative and flexible home-based business. Does it take work? Of course, but it is worth it. Many spouses just need to realize that network marketing isn't some "quacky scheme," but a unique way to live the life of their dreams. In fact, far from being a bad business decision, networking has been validated by the most conservative and successful investor in American history. Warren Buffet, the "Oracle of Omaha," has been buying network marketing and direct sales companies for a few years now. So as a spouse of someone in network marketing, you are in good company when you support your spouse in his or her work.

- What you say to your spouse—and how you say it—plays a huge role in how your spouse responds to you and how they work in their business. It came to a crucial point for the Fasons when Robert literally walked out of the house and said he couldn't take the negativity anymore. There is an old proverb I am reminded of that says, "The tongue has the power of life and death." That is so true! Have you ever realized that the words that you speak to your spouse have the power to infuse life into him or her? Did you know that the words you speak can literally change your spouse's chemical balance? It is true. Imagine walking into your house and seeing that your wife has been to the hairstylist that day. And you say, "What in the world happened to your hair?" How is *that* going to go over? Not well! But if you say, "WOW! You look fantastic!" you will get a different response altogether. In each case, your wife's mind will produce chemicals that tell her to experience sadness and rejection, or happiness and joy. That is the power you have to encourage your spouse. Take it seriously! Speak life to your spouse and you will watch him or her soar.

- Ultimately you must make a choice to grow as a person. Donna had to commit to her own program of personal development. And when she grew, she became an asset to Robert's business, rather than a liability. It's like one of my mentors, Jim Rohn, has always said:

"Work harder on yourself than you do on your job." This applies to anything, really. We need to work harder on ourselves than anything else. *We* are the key component to change. What are you doing to grow yourself? What books and audio programs are you listening to? How are you improving yourself? As you grow, you will see a whole new world open up, and you will see your relationship with your spouse grow as well.

If you follow the advice of this book—to work hard, to become positive, to support your spouse, to get on a plan of personal growth, to do *Whatever It Takes*—you will begin to see success come into your life, and you'll begin to enjoy its benefits. The stories Donna tells about the trips and experiences their family has had is the end result of doing the work to become successful. Living life as Donna describes it will put you and your spouse on an amazing journey of self-improvement, success, family togetherness, and joyful living. Through network marketing you can be involved with great people, products, and services. You can achieve financial and time freedom. You can, as the title of one of my books says, *Live the Life You Have Always Dreamed Of.*

Will it take work? Yes.
Will there be ups and downs? Yes.
Will you feel like quitting from time to time? Yes.

Will it be worth it for your finances and your family? Absolutely!

But only if you do.... *Whatever It Takes!*

My wishes for total success for you and your family!

Chris Widener
www.ChrisWidener.com

PREFACE

et me introduce myself. My name is Donna Fason and I'm from Mt. Vernon, Arkansas. I married my high school sweetheart, Robert Fason, over twenty-seven years ago. We have two children: Joni, age 24, and Cody, age 17.

Robert and I both grew up on dairy farms in the same part of Arkansas where we live now. After getting married right out of high school, we got into the dairy business ourselves. We managed to struggle through about six years of farming before going broke, being forced to auction off all of our cattle and the equipment we had worked so hard for. Robert ended up back on a dairy farm, working for my dad. I went to work in a factory. Then we spent a couple of years working for some friends of ours who owned their own business. Robert was in sales and I was a secretary.

During that time, we were introduced to direct sales and network marketing. We started out on a part-time basis just to earn an extra hundred dollars a week.

As it turned out, within a couple of

years, we were earning more part-time with network marketing than we were making full-time with both of us working.

So, we reevaluated this new concept called "network marketing," and decided to make a five-year commitment, to do **Whatever It Takes!** and go full-time.

I am a mom first and when this decision was made, Cody was just a few months old, so we decided that Robert would work the business and I would stay home and raise our children. For the past seventeen years, I've seen a lot and have certainly learned a lot about supporting and not supporting your spouse in network marketing.

Now that our children are older—and we've finally succeeded and can now afford for both of us to travel—we work our network marketing business together as a team. We travel all over the United States, sharing with people everywhere our story and teaching them how to succeed in our business.

Network marketing is very different from the traditional ways of doing business. I find many people have a hard time grasping the concept and when they do, it's usually just one spouse who gets it. The husband or wife is excited and ready to go, while their partner is not as excited and really can't understand why the other one is.

The spouse who isn't enthusiastic is more concerned with *why* instead of *what* has their spouse so excited.

They see that something else is taking their spouse's focus and free time, plus their partner may be having fun, and none of this has to do with them or their family. A red flag is raised... a wall starts going up... maybe there's a little bit of jealousy... and the problems begin.

Been there and done with that!

I've started sharing how I learned to deal with understanding network marketing from a spouse's point of view. The company we are with has even produced a video and audio of one of my talks. I have people everywhere tell me, "I wish my partner was here!" Or they say, "Thank you Donna, you've really helped me to understand." People tell me, "Your tape really helped my spouse and me."

After months of that kind of response, I realized I have so much more to give than time allows on stage. I decided to write this book, in hopes of helping more people. After all, the concept of network marketing is people helping people. It's about making a difference in other people's lives. It's about doing Whatever It Takes!

If I can make a difference for you, then I've succeeded. If I can make a difference for you, then you can make a difference for someone else.

I dedicate this book to *you*. You do make a difference—you are my inspiration!

WHAT IS NETWORK MARKETING?

*I would rather have one percent of 100 people's efforts,
than 100 percent of my own.*

— *Andrew Carnegie*

First, I'm going to describe what network marketing appears to be from a typical spouse's point of view. Then I'll share with you what it *really* is, once the blinders are off.

This was something I struggled with for years. I was very unhappy and miserable, because I just didn't understand—nor did I want to understand—this thing called network marketing.

I saw it as a threat to my marriage. Network marketing took my husband away from our kids and me. It was something that ate up any extra income from our family.

The jealousy I felt toward all things network marketing had me so miserable I lost all my self-esteem. I was almost in a state of depression. I even lost the only thing I thought never could be taken away from me... and that was to be a good mother to my kids.

Children are so innocent; they don't have a clue about life and work. I would find myself telling my daughter, "I would if I could..." or "We can't afford it right now." And at the same time, Robert would be spending money on gas or meals to do his network marketing business. I couldn't understand why we were doing without, while he was out having fun (or so I thought at the time).

We had one decent vehicle and guess what? Robert had it all the time. Even if I did manage to land a job that would pay enough to cover day-care for two kids, gas, lunch, and a halfway decent wardrobe, I didn't even have a car to get me there.

Another issue was that Robert and I both made the commitment to go full-time, so if I did get a job, what would that do for the network marketing business we'd started? Robert was working day and night, traveling and sharing with people how to make a living in network marketing. His belief was so strong that we would succeed; my taking a job would not only damage his credibility in our business, but would destroy him as well.

I had no control over anything. Network marketing was ruining my life; I didn't want any part of it.

Since I wasn't involved in the business and had no idea when or how much money I would have to spend on our kids, I couldn't tell them when we could go to McDonald's or when I could take them to the zoo. I didn't have any of the answers they wanted to hear, so I felt I couldn't even be a mommy for my kids. I felt totally helpless and useless. I hated what I thought network marketing had done to me... to all of us.

Because I didn't *know* what network marketing was all about, I saw it as something that came between my relationship with me and my husband. I saw it as one great big negative in my life.

I did figure out, though, that being negative around people at our network marketing events was not a good thing. Robert and I had argued enough about this that when I did have the opportunity to attend an event with him, I just kept my mouth shut. I knew if I did say something negative, he would probably not take me with him the next time. And I did enjoy the times we got to make trips together. We got to spend time together, and I desperately needed that time with him to realize that he did love me.

The more I started traveling with him, the more I learned about network marketing. Our business started growing and we started to succeed. Our roller-coaster income started to level out and then to grow each and every month. We were finally seeing the results of a four-and-a-half-year struggle.

We had finally made it to the top of the company we were with. When you are at the top, your name gets out; people want to know how you did it.

We had become an overnight success— in four and a half years!

There are literally thousands of network marketing companies out there and new ones starting up every day. Once we had succeeded and people knew who we were and how successful we'd become, network marketers from other companies were calling us all the time, sending us videos and literature, trying to recruit us into their "opportunity."

They would say, "You made it with that company, you'll make a fortune with us." I have a whole file cabinet full of other deals, 90 percent of which are probably no longer in business.

Sure, we glanced through their stuff, but we were so happy that we were finally making money that it was really hard to even think about doing anything else. We did, however, take a look at one company about nine years ago, and for several reasons, we made the decision to resign from the company we were with and join our present company. We started part-time and within thirty days decided to go full-time. That proved to be a wise and very profitable decision for us.

Some people have said that it must have taken a lot of courage to walk away from a $150,000 annual income. Not really. We were making good money, but our people weren't. When we saw a way that others could succeed with less people involved and in a lot less time, we knew we could replace our income if we just went to work.

We started with our friends and neighbors who were not involved with our previous company. The first month we more than replaced our own income, but more importantly our people began making money.

Was it hard to make that decision?

When I realized that Robert was serious about looking at another company and going to an event to learn more, I told him, "Fine, go on and get it out of your system," so he could get back to work, doing what we knew. I was not open to looking at something else. As I went to bed that night I said a little prayer, because I was nervous about walking away from our current income. I ask God to make it so silly he would know it wasn't for him and get right back to our previous business—or to make it so strong that he would know for sure this was something we had to do.

The next day Robert called me so excited; I could hear it in his voice that he was going to do this. It had to be powerful to make him walk away from what we had built for those eight and a half years. My prayer was answered. The decision was easy!

How did I feel?

Excited about the opportunity. Nervous about learning the business fast enough so we wouldn't have to miss a paycheck. I agreed to come over to the event and learn what I could, mostly because I planned on telling Robert what to do, not because I wanted to work the business. As it turned out, I liked what I saw and started out right away helping a lot more than I had planned.

The company, the product, and the pay plan are all major factors in your success with network marketing. But just as important is you. Our claim to success is not that we were naturals; we paid our dues long before we ever knew about the company we're involved with now. I'll share some of those dues-paying (struggles and personal growth) stories with you later in the book.

But first, I want to share with you what I have learned—the real truth about network marketing.

Network marketing is, simply put, people helping people to succeed in business.

The concept of network marketing has been around for years.

Let me give you an example of how it works: I go to a new restaurant; the food, the service, the atmosphere, everything, is great. I tell you about it and you go there, too. I have just networked with you for that restaurant. It's sharing with others something good, kind of like a referral.

The only difference is that the restaurant didn't send me any money for referring you, but by referring you to my network marketing business, when you buy or sell a product, the company does send me money.

People network every day and don't even realize it—and they're not getting paid for it, but they could be.

Maybe you tell someone about a great movie or a sale at a dress shop; you have just networked with them. It's a pretty neat concept—and most people do it every day of their lives!

In network marketing, the key elements are the company, the products, and the pay plan, which explains how you earn money by moving the products and helping others do the same. You will usually earn a direct sales commission for individual referrals or sales. You will then earn bonus commissions or overrides from referrals or sales made by the people who have joined you in your network marketing business. As your team grows, so do your bonuses and overrides. Once again, it's all about people helping people to succeed.

To help you feel a little more comfortable with supporting your partner in their business, ask your spouse these two questions. We've found these to be major factors in selecting the right company and sharing it with our friends for long-term commitment and success:

1. **Is the company at least five years old?**

2. **Would I use the products if there were no money to be made?**

I'm not saying that new companies can't or won't succeed, but according to some studies done on this industry, not many will make it past the one- to two-year mark.

However, if they do make it past five years, their chances of being here for the long haul are much greater. Fortunately, it has never happened to us—we've only been with two companies—but I have heard a lot of nightmares out there, where people have gotten involved and worked hard only to have the company go out of business in less than two years. I see a lot of skepticism from folks because of this. The main thing is that you need to feel good about what you are doing before you can share it with others.

One of my favorite things about network marketing is the opportunity to potentially earn above an average income, without prior experience and without educational qualifications.

That means everyone can do it, regardless of background and regardless of age—even a couple of ex-broke dairy farmers with only high school educations.

Wow! What an opportunity!

The three key ingredients we have found that it takes to succeed are:

a desire to succeed
a willingness to work
and being teachable.

I've seen folks from all walks of life earning outrageous incomes in network marketing.

Everyone doesn't succeed, but don't knock it until you try it!

Here's our track record with network marketing:

- In the first four and a half years, we earned just enough money to cover our bare essential expenses.

- Over the next four years, we averaged per month what we would have earned in a year in the dairy business.

- During the next year, we averaged per month what we would have earned in two years in the dairy business.

- We now earn more per month than we would have earned in four full years in the dairy business and our business is consistently growing.

You tell me, which would you rather do—milk cows for four years or work your network marketing business for one month?

I will admit, the first four and a half years weren't very pretty around my house, and I wasn't very excited about network marketing or very supportive. But I can say now, after seventeen years and many, many, *many* dreams and goals becoming realities, my attitude and my involvement with network marketing has definitely and dramatically changed.

My Spouse Is Not the Same Person

Until you make peace with who you are, you'll never be content with what you have.

— *Doris Morton*

D o you ever feel like your spouse has changed due to being involved in network marketing?

Do you ever wonder, "Where is the person I married?"

Do you ever feel like your relationship with your spouse has taken a turn for the worse?

Do your friends ever ask you what's wrong with your spouse?

I've said Yes to all the above! Boy, did I ever!

Most of us are not so fortunate as to be rich when our spouses get involved with network marketing. That's usually the reason people get involved in the first place—to make money. I know that's why we got into the business.

We got involved—with my approval—to earn an extra hundred dollars a week. I had no idea that I would have to go

through the struggles that lay ahead.

With two small children at home and not enough money to afford baby-sitting and the expenses of my tagging along with him, Robert made a five-year commitment and went out to work our network marketing business. Working the business meant talking to people, sharing our products, and attending meetings.

Our company used a weekly meeting as a way for people like us to bring our guests to hear someone more experienced in the business share the opportunity. Plus, to better serve the masses, most of these meetings were held at night, so people who worked full-time jobs could attend.

A lot of times, dinner was included. The meetings were either held at a restaurant or we offered to buy dinner for our guests in order to get them to come to the meeting. This didn't bother me too much in the beginning, but then came the trainings and big events, which usually were held out of town. That meant travel expenses, not to mention the fee for the training itself. Does any of this sound familiar?

Here I was, at home with two kids, and I didn't have a clue as to what went on at these so-called meetings and events. All I could see is that my spouse was happy, having fun, eating at nice restaurants, and staying in nice hotels. People were calling my house for him all the time, and a lot of them were females whom I didn't know, and so I started to feel a little bit jealous.

I did get the opportunity to attend a few of the big events and was greeted with...

"Oh, so *you're* Robert's wife," and I have to tell you, that didn't go over too well with me at all.

Our bills were piling up. I told my kids, "I would if I could," so many times it wasn't funny—it was downright sad. The only thing I could see about network marketing was that my husband was having the time of his life while our kids and I were doing without and feeling miserable.

Robert refused to discuss any financial problems we were having. If we ever started a conversation on money, it ended up in an argument and he flatly refused to discuss it. He would always end the conversation with, "Don't worry about it, everything's great," and then leave the room to do something else.

Since I was the one at home, I had to answer all the phone calls from creditors. I had to beg the utility companies to give us a little while longer to pay the bills. I was the one making the promises; yet he was the one in control of the money. Did I worry? All the time.

My self-esteem had gotten so low that there were times when I would stay in bed all day.

I felt my husband had a new life now, which obviously didn't include me. I couldn't give my kids the answers they wanted to hear about when things would get better; it was all me, all my fault that my family was falling apart.

I wasn't a good wife; we argued all the time.

I wasn't a good mother; I couldn't give my kids the things they wanted. I had no control over anything in my life.

I felt totally helpless and useless.

I had finally hit bottom.

It was a normal day, as normal as it could be back then.

Creditors calling...all day long, and me making promises to them I knew I couldn't keep. That day, our daughter Joni came home from school so excited about the upcoming school celebration. She said, "Mommy, can I please be in the pageant?"

I had to try and explain to my little girl with tears in my eyes how expensive it was to get a dress; the entry fee and additional costs would be over a hundred dollars that I just did not have... "But I would if I could."

With sadness in her eyes Joni replied, "It's OK, Mommy, I understand."

This was more than I could handle. Something had to give somewhere, somehow. We had struggled like this for almost four years with this thing called network marketing, and I was fed up. I didn't care what it took—when Robert got home that evening, he was going to listen to me.... He was going to give me answers, not just another, "Don't worry, honey, everything's great."

I wanted to know the date that we were going to make it; I needed to know when could I stop worrying. I could no longer handle the wishing—I wanted answers now!

I watched my husband pull up in the driveway, and I was ready to let him have it. He was not going to ignore the issue this time!

He opened the door and stepped into the kitchen, all smiles as usual. I started in about the creditors... about the kids... how miserable I was... and I demanded answers, now!

And then he did something that I had never dreamed he would do.

We had been together since junior high school; it was always Robert and Donna or Donna and Robert. He looked me straight in the eyes, put both hands on each side of his head like blinders on a horse, and said,

"Baby, I love you, but if we're ever going to succeed, I can't listen to this negativity."

He turned around. Walked out the door. Got back in the car and drove away.

My husband had just walked out on me.

I was speechless; I could not believe what had just happened. I was deeply hurt. Separation or divorce was something neither of us believed was ever an option for us. We had always agreed we'd get through things together no matter what...**Whatever It Takes!** But there I sat. He was gone, and I did nothing to try and stop him.

Everything bad went racing through my mind: maybe he had found someone else; after all, he had been gone a lot lately. Maybe I drove him away, because I had not been very supportive of him or his business. So there I was, blaming myself again.

The longer I sat and thought, the more I decided it wasn't my fault. Then I got angry... very angry.

All I had wanted was for him to listen to what I had to say for a change. And he couldn't even give me the courtesy of listening. So, I sat alone and screamed; I yelled, I cried, I yelled some more, I cried some more, and then I felt hurt again. My emotions were crazy, ranging from angry, sad, angry, sad... back and forth until I realized it was getting late and he wasn't home yet.

Was he coming back? I had no idea.

I decided to go lie down and try and figure out what I was I going to do next.

I heard the car pull up, and I started trying to imagine what he was thinking by now. Was he thinking: *Maybe she's cooled down by now.* Or was he thinking: *This is my house and I don't have to go anywhere.* Or what?

I thought, *I just wanted him to listen to me, but I'm afraid if I say anything he may leave again, and I know I don't want that.*

He walked into the bedroom, noticed that I was awake, but we didn't say a word to each other. He got into bed and—just like a man—went to sleep almost instantly. (I'm sure if you're a woman, you'll agree with me, men can just fall fast asleep like that as if nothing ever happened.)

This made me angry again, but I didn't say a word.

Then I grabbed the remote control; it was late at night, I couldn't sleep, and I couldn't concentrate, so I just flipped through the channels. And as I flipped through the channels, something caught my eye: an infomercial with Anthony Robbins. I watched and listened.

The speakers at the few events I had attended with Robert always taught us to listen to motivational tapes or read motivational books. I had heard them say it, but I assumed they were talking to the people who were working the business, not me. This infomercial was about motivation, but not about network marketing.

Tony Robbins was talking to *me*. He was talking about becoming a better person. I was desperate to change. I did not like the person I had become.

I wrote down the phone number, slipped out of bed, went to the kitchen, got out my credit cards and called the companies for our available credit balances. I found one that I could use—our Discover card (which I proudly refer to now as my Recover card). It had an available credit of $210.00. The tapes that were going to change my life cost $179.00.

It was a twenty-four-day program consisting of twelve tapes; if I listened to one side per day, my life could change. It only took thirty minutes per day.

Anthony Robbins said that whatever you wanted to change in your life, you could change with this program: You could have a better relationship with your spouse, become a better parent, lose weight, and get physically fit. Whatever you wanted, you could have it if you followed his program.

In my mind, he was saying, "Donna Fason definitely needs this," so I ordered it.

As I waited for the tapes to arrive, I thought, *I need to focus on what it is I want from this program.* Improving my relationship with my spouse would mean both of us working at it; we still could just barely carry on a conversation without an argument, so I wasn't ready for that without Robert's support. Plus, I would have to tell him that I had just spent almost two hundred dollars that we didn't have. Being a better parent—well, I still didn't have the answers my kids wanted to hear; that too, would include Robert.

So, I decided that I could focus on losing weight and getting physically fit, and no one would know what I was doing. If it worked, I could go through it again with another focus.

I anxiously awaited the arrival of this new program that was going to change my life. I was finally going to do something that I did have control over, and that was to lose weight. I already felt better, just knowing they were coming.

On the day my tapes arrived, I was actually happy that Robert wasn't home. Now I wouldn't have to explain what I had ordered and why, and I could go ahead and get started changing for the better right away.

I could feel a shift in myself the very first day. It was like a weight had been lifted; there was light at the end of the tunnel.

I could hardly wait each day for Robert to go work his business so I could listen to my tapes. Each day I learned more and more. I started finding the answers for all the things that had gone wrong. Robert had been listening to motivational tapes, like he had been taught. I always thought they were to help him in his network marketing business, not to help him to become a better person. I hadn't yet realized those two things were one and the same.

Being your own boss and succeeding in network marketing requires a lot of belief in yourself; I just didn't realize it at the time.

Each day I realized more and more why Robert did the things he did. I realized that I had become a negative for him, and until his belief in himself was strong enough, he had to stay away from negatives like me. Robert had quit watching TV, he had quit reading the newspaper, and he had quit socializing with our mostly negative friends.

I thought he was just so caught up in his business that he didn't have time for any of this anymore. I also thought he was becoming too good for us. He was a big shot network marketer, who owned his own business. He was a bigwig.

Since I didn't work with him in the business, I had plenty of time to watch TV and read the paper. And I desperately needed friends. I finally realized that this was why we couldn't communicate.

I was continuing to be surrounded with negatives while he was surrounding himself with positives. They just don't mix—one will win over the other.

I began to realize that he was only doing what he needed to do for us to ever get ahead in life and get out of the financial mess we had gotten into.

No, we haven't totally given up TV, newspapers, or our friends. We have just learned how to use all these as positives in our lives. We still like to see a good movie now and then. We do read positive articles in the paper, and like to see our kids' names listed on their school honor roll, or mentioned in ball games, etc.

And yes, we are still friends with all of our old friends. We still keep in touch. We have total respect for our friends, as they do for us, even though we all have different dreams and goals. It was tough for a while, but we all realize now what each of us wants in life, we understand the changes in our relationships, and we respect each other for who we are.

Your friends can be touchy about your relationship with them. Sometimes they feel the same way toward you when your attitude changes to a more positive one as I felt towards Robert's behavior.

Just stay focused on your goals; true friends are still there!

Our true friends never knocked what we were doing; they just strongly felt that they couldn't do network marketing themselves. And some of them have since joined us in our network marketing business and are now going through some of the same things that we did. Even though the struggles we went through were tough, our experiences have allowed us to help our friends through their own struggles a lot more quickly and experience success a lot sooner.

If we had continued to listen to others' suggestions of not being able to succeed, we would have soon seen ourselves as failures. As hard as it seems to walk away with your blinders on—and I can only imagine how hard it was for Robert to walk away from me that night—that's what you have to do if you want things to change.

Your friends may not understand at first, but just like me, they will later.

I've learned that you can't change someone else; you just accept them for who they are and move on.

The old saying, "It's OK if they don't buy your story as long as you don't buy theirs," really does mean a lot. Once your belief in yourself is strong enough to overcome any objections, you will succeed and you'll find that your friends are still your friends.

We had to stop and think, *We're in this business full-time.* We had to focus on what was right for us. If we wanted to succeed like the people we saw in the front of the room, up on stage, we had to do what they were teaching us to do. If that meant spending a weekend at a training seminar instead of spending a weekend of leisure with our friends, then that's what we had to do. After all, neither of us had a job or an education to fall back on for income.

We had to develop a "Whatever It Takes!" attitude. And we did!

I learned to set goals and to achieve them. I learned that you can have what you want from life. Before long, Robert and I were talking without arguing. Our relationship was healing; things were finally changing in my life for the better. My life and my future looked so much brighter, and all I did was listen to a 30-minute tape each day.

Yes, I did lose weight, and yes, I did become a better mother. I was happy for a change!

I want you to realize what happened to me—I changed my way of thinking. None of my circumstances changed, my kids still wanted things we couldn't afford, the bill collectors kept calling, and our business did not explode that very day or the next for that matter. But what I learned was how to change my way of thinking on a daily basis.

I had been looking for the answers to my problems in all the wrong places.

My old thinking was that if the kids wouldn't ask for something, I wouldn't be upset that I couldn't give it to them. If the bill collectors wouldn't call, I wouldn't be angry that they had. And if Robert would go ahead and get our business to take off, I wouldn't be disappointed each day when it didn't happen.

I began learning the process and the power of positive thinking.

For things to change for me, I had to change.

That's easy for me to say now, because I've lived through it and survived, and my family has survived. But remember, it wasn't easy for me to get to this point.

If you're experiencing similar thoughts and situations, how can I get you to understand how important reading motivational books is for you as a spouse?

Most of us weren't taught this in school; we don't realize how positive thinking can improve our lives on a daily basis.

I was, however, excited to learn that our schools are now encouraging our kids in this area. At our children's school a couple of years ago, I saw up on the bulletin board in the hall a huge poster titled, "To Achieve Your Dreams, Remember Your ABCs." I had not seen this before and was so touched by it; I ran back to the car to grab a notepad and pen so I could write it all down. Here's what was up on that board:

Avoid negative sources, people, places, things and habits.

Believe in yourself.

Consider things from every angle.

I've also been told by one of my nieces that every freshman entering one of the classes at the local college is required to read the book *Tuesdays with Morrie*. I have that book, and it is very motivational. We're also seeing a lot of this in the corporate world. Big-name motivational speakers are traveling the world to speak at seminars for corporate sales teams and leaders.

But how do you know if you've never been exposed to any of this?

All I can ask of you is to trust me and try it. I don't necessarily recommend one author over another. The key is to get a book in your hand and read it or a tape in your player and listen to it. I prefer some books over others because I can relate more to them and understand them.

I enjoy inspirational as well as motivational books. I have in my personal library almost every *Chicken Soup for the Soul* book in the series. I have subscriptions to *Guideposts* and *Angels on Earth*, and each time a new issue arrives, I sit right down that night and read it before I go to bed.

Motivational and inspirational books tell true stories about people's lives. They help us to get through our own day-to-day struggles by sharing stories of how others got through their struggles.

Through my reading, I learned that I wasn't the only person in the world to ever feel down and out. There are thousands of books out there—just start reading.

Have you ever shared a story with a friend about your child misbehaving in public and how embarrassed you were, and then your friend came back with a similar story about their child? Even though you didn't feel better about your child's behavior, you felt better knowing that your child wasn't the only one to misbehave. And you were relieved to know that you weren't the only person in the world to ever experience such an event. That's how books and tapes can help you.

At one point in my life, I had been happy; I was on top of the world from elementary to high school to graduating, getting married, starting our own business and raising a family. Everything was going according to plan, I was moving on with my life, and I was living my dreams! I don't know when, where, why or how I ended up at the point that I did.

Somewhere amidst the responsibilities of running a household, managing a home-based business, and being a parent while struggling to get by financially, I quit dreaming. I started thinking survival instead of getting ahead in life.

I didn't realize it then, but I certainly do know now just how true Earl Nightingale's quote, "You become what you think about," really is.

We all have secrets in our lives, things that we struggle with by ourselves. We tell ourselves things will get better, but guess what? They don't get any better until we do something to make them better.

Our financial struggles were our private business; they were our secret. I would have died before I would have let our parents and families and friends know how bad it really was.

Our arguments were nobody else's business, either. I wouldn't dare let anybody know there were problems in our house. I was already feeling enough like a failure, and the last thing I wanted to hear was, "I told you so." Robert had approached some of these people with his network marketing business, and they had laughed at him and blew him off.

Seeing that program on TV rather than at a business function really hit home with me. It gave me hope and made me realize the importance of believing in myself. It showed me how just a few minutes each day could change my life. Remember, at that time in my life I wasn't close to being a network marketer, nor was I ever looking to become one. I just wanted to be happy again. I just wanted answers to my problems.

I'm not telling you to read books so that you'll join your spouse in his or her network marketing business.

I'm telling you to read books so that you can understand where your spouse is coming from when they act like somebody you've never met.

Once you've tried reading motivational books, your belief in yourself will get stronger. It doesn't matter how strong you think you are. We all need to be pumped up on a daily basis.

Once you're reading these books, you will find yourself dreaming and thinking, *What if?* You may even set some goals of your own and achieve them. And the next thing you know, you will be doing things you thought you'd never do.

You might find yourself wearing that outfit or suit that looks better on you than it did on the model in the magazine. You might just go ahead, take off and play basketball with the kids, something that you haven't done in years. And, if you're like most people who are really busy, you just might find yourself relaxing and enjoying that one-hour massage at the spa, because you deserve it!

You just might find yourself waking up one morning and saying, *"Wow,* isn't life great!"

I didn't read books and listen to tapes to get involved with network marketing. I read books and listened to tapes to feel better about myself and to believe in myself again.

It was still a few years before I began to get interested in my husband's business. From what I had learned about personal growth and belief in myself, I found myself wanting to become involved in Robert's business with him.

It had been our business all along; I just never looked at it that way before. Now I knew: this truly was our business.

Always Feel Great!

Dost thou love life? Then do not squander time,
for that is the stuff that life is made of.

— Benjamin Franklin

Once you've understood what your spouse is doing with network marketing and you've listened to something motivational to understand what positive thinking is all about, you will need to learn that no matter what, *always feel GREAT!*

I know that there's a time and a place for everything. I know life can't always be great; you will have bad days. People with positive attitudes do have bad days, but we just don't see them. We think that they are always happy and everything is perfect for them.

I felt that way about Robert before I understood the power of positive thinking. He never let me see him down and he never talked to me about his problems, because he knew I was already about as low mentally as a person could get. When Robert needed to feel better, he would go to events and meetings where people were positive and let their positive attitudes rub off on him.

I learned about always feeling great from other spouses in

our business that had more experience than I did.

Once we were at a big event and during one of the breaks, I just asked one of the wives, "How do you do it?" She asked me, "What?" I said, "How do you keep going and how can you be so happy when you are the one home with the kids all day, every day, taking all the phone calls, keeping the house, doing all the laundry, the cooking, the errands, the paperwork, ordering products and other details of your network marketing business—when all your spouse does is travel, eat in nice restaurants and have fun?

How do you deal with that and yet feel great about it? I think we spouses are getting the wrong end of this deal!"

Her reply was, "Donna, think about all the hours that Robert spends away from you and your kids. Think about all the ball games and fun stuff for your kids that he misses. Think about all the late nights when he's tired and still three hours away from home."

She also said, "Donna, Robert wants to be home and spend more time with you and the kids, but if he intends to build any kind of a future for you and your family, he has to do whatever it takes now to build his business. To build and develop leaders within network marketing does require traveling to teach others to duplicate his efforts. Once he has others trained to do what he does, he will be able to be home more and spend more time with your family."

There it was again: "Whatever It Takes!"

I had to realize that our business was growing, we were helping others, and in return our income was growing to justify all the hard work that Robert was doing.

Robert's goal was not just to pay the bills, but also to help enough other people get what they wanted so that we as a family could have everything we wanted.

He was doing this so that we all could have a better future.

I got the opportunity a few weeks later to show him how I, too, could feel great.

It was another normal day at the Fason house: Robert left early to go work his business with presentations all day long, the last one being about three hours away from home. It was late, about midnight, and I had just settled into my recliner to watch a movie when the phone rang. It was Robert, and the first thing out of his mouth was, "How was your day?"

Remembering that I needed to be supportive I said, "*Great!*" With surprise in his voice he said, "Really, what did you do today?"

At this time, Joni was ten years old and Cody was only three. Here was my answer to Robert:

Well, we woke up around 9:00 a.m. and you know that stomach virus that's going around? Well, Cody has it. He woke up with a 103-degree temperature, vomiting and diarrhea every fifteen minutes. By the time I got one mess cleaned up, there he'd go again. That went on for several hours.

And, oh yeah, remember Joni was going to a friend's house today for a slumber party? I got a phone call around 5:00 p.m. saying they had all gone swimming and were riding home in the back of a pickup truck, sitting on the tailgate

with their wet suits on and driving down the road and Joni
slipped off the tailgate onto the pavement and was scraped
up pretty bad. They said I should come pick her up right
away and take her to the emergency room.

So I called my sister to keep Cody while I went to get Joni.
My sister made her husband—who always runs from anyone
who's sick—keep Cody, so she could help me with Joni. We got
to the hospital; they took X-rays—no broken bones. So they
sent us to the waiting room for four hours.

When we finally saw a doctor, he treated the scrapes like they
were burns, wrapped Joni up like a mummy, and we went
home. I got her settled, and then went to pick up Cody.

By this time, he was much better; no fever, no more vomiting
or diarrhea, so I got him settled in bed. Then I kicked back in
the recliner to relax—we've been home about fifteen minutes.

Other than that, my day's been GREAT! How was your day?

There was dead silence on the other end of the phone and I
was thinking, _Silly cell phones, we got disconnected and I've
been rattling on for five minutes to nobody._

I said, "Hello, hello?" Then finally I heard, "_Wow!_ You did all
of that and your day was great?" Again, with a very excited
voice, I said to Robert, "Yes, how was your day?"

Well, naturally he was going to say, "Great!" no matter how
his day went. Most husbands, especially mine, would rather
take a beating than to go through what I did that day. If I
could still feel great after all that, even if his day had been
terrible, he wouldn't admit it, so he said his day was great
too.

It's all in your attitude. It's not what happens to you, but how you react to what happens to you.

I finally understood what a positive attitude was all about. When bad days happen, and they will, we do have a choice.

We can have a bad day and continue to feel bad, or we can have a bad day and end it feeling great.

Either way, a bad day is a bad day. Personally, I like a great day!

I want you to try this sometime when things don't go as planned and you have a bad day: When you go to bed at night tell yourself, *I feel **great**!* Really mean it. Forget about whatever happened; tomorrow is another day. Just tell yourself, *I feel great,* over and over until you really do feel great. I promise, you will rest better, tomorrow will be a much better day, and you will be a happier person.

I hear this all the time and I've read it in several books: If whatever has upset me won't make a difference in one, five, or ten years from now, why let it bother me now? Blow it off and move on! Life is too short and too precious to not enjoy it.

I have a sign by my telephone in big letters that reads, "GREAT!" I keep it there to remind me how much that one word can make a difference in other people's lives. Here's a quick story on that:

I'm not a morning person. One morning, I got up and walked to the kitchen still half asleep, when my phone rang. Now, I should know better than to answer the phone until I am fully awake, but I answered it anyway. It was someone in our network marketing business and they asked me how I was doing.

I answered sleepily, "I'm OK." Immediately, I heard the tone of the person's voice drop about three notches. People were so used to my *great* attitude, that to hear me any other way was a little discouraging for them. I felt badly because I realized that my attitude had changed that person's attitude. Just because I was groggy or irritable was no reason to make someone else feel bad. That will never happen again!

Try using the word *great* in your vocabulary every day as much as possible. See what responses you get from people when you say, "Great!"

Robert went through McDonald's one morning and, as usual, the young girl at the window asked him how he was doing. His response, of course, was, "Great!"

She looked at him and a big smile came across her face as she said, "You don't have to work today, right?" He said that he was working, and as she handed him his order, she just kept smiling. She may have thought he was crazy, but it sure put a smile on her face and brightened up her day.

Tell a coworker, "You look great!" Tell your children, "You did a great job!" Notice how much it raises their spirits. Try it on your spouse when he or she has just returned home from a meeting, and even though he or she is really afraid of your response, asks about your day anyway, just to start up a great! conversation. You'll be surprised at how much closer your relationship will get.

It didn't really matter that, at the time, I did not work our network marketing business with Robert. At least now we could carry on a conversation without an argument. We could communicate again. That was what I had wanted all along, and now I understood how I could accomplish it. Now we could start discussing our finances. We knew where each other was coming from, and we began working together instead of against each other to make a plan to get us out of our mess.

I want you to think about this, please:

All I did was change my attitude by adding the word *great!* and *really* meaning it.

That one little word can change everything.

Over 100 of our team's leaders on our houseboat named, Whatever It Takes.

You and Your Spouse BOTH Need Support

Give others a piece of your heart, not a piece of your mind.

— Author Unknown

If you are a parent, I'm sure you have days with your kids that are pretty stressful. By the day's end, it would help your feelings tremendously if your partner would share a cup of coffee, relax on the sofa, or snuggle in bed and reassure you things will be OK, things will get better. We all go through times when we need a shoulder to lean on, and the most comforting shoulder is that of a spouse. We all need to feel loved and appreciated.

I had finally accepted the fact that Robert was going to do network marketing, with or without me. After discussing our finances and looking into all the other income possibilities, it did make sense.

If Robert put the hours into network marketing that he would have to put into a job, he could make much more money.

But could he work for himself as the boss? I knew he was gone a lot and on the phone a lot. He always said he was working, but I sure couldn't tell it by the income.

After going through the motivational tapes, learning how to have a great attitude, and beginning to share our day's events with each other again, it finally hit me! Robert was working his network marketing business, but why wasn't he making the money to compensate for the hours he was working?

Network marketing is a numbers game.

Network marketing is a people-helping-people business and Robert just hadn't talked to enough people yet to find the ones who really wanted it.

Little did we know, after four and a half years we were almost home!

We had worked for six months promoting a major company event. Our sponsor had told us that if we had twenty people there, our business would explode. Well, I was way past ready for that explosion, so I started doing what I could to help.

We finally had twenty people make the commitment to attend. We left late at night for our eight-hour drive so we could arrive first thing the next morning when the event started, saving the hotel charge for one night. I was beginning to get excited; our business was going to explode! We registered for the event and began to look around for those twenty people who committed to coming.

We couldn't find one person.

We went ahead and sat in on the events, thinking, *Maybe we just missed them; surely we'd run into them before the day*

was over. For two and a half days we searched the crowds—
still, no one. Not one of the twenty showed up. We were
terribly disappointed and let down.

As we listened to the speakers and heard the stories from
people ranging in age from eighteen to ninety, many of whom
had only been in network marketing for six months or less
and had already earned unreal amounts of money, we got
more upset. I saw that Robert was really down. I had never
seen him like this, and it scared me.

As we started our long drive home, he quit network marketing. He said,

"I give up. I'm just not cut out for this. I've done everything I've been taught and it's just not working. I don't know what else to do."

Right away, I started getting really nervous about our future.
I was trying to think of what I could say to help Robert. We
began to discuss things we had learned from the event. One
speaker said, "The only way you can lose is to quit. Don't ever
quit!" Another speaker said, "You ain't gonna make it with
the ones you got!" Obviously, not with the ones we had! Then
we discussed the success stories we had heard. Those people
were no different than us; if they could do it, so could we!

I told him, "You've never quit anything that you set your
mind to do, and besides that, you told me you were committed to five years and it has only been four and a half, so you
can't quit!"

I don't think anyone else besides me as his spouse could
have given him the support that he needed to continue on at
that moment. I knew that a shoulder to lean on, to be able to
vent his feelings from a bad weekend, and a great attitude to

support him and encourage him could get him back on track.

Ever since we had learned how to communicate again without arguments, we could also cheer each other up. Robert definitely needed some cheering up. I had enough belief in him and what he was doing to not want to let this one go.

We discussed each other's feelings about the weekend and gave each other the strength and the confidence to succeed. We set a game plan and went to work.

Before we arrived back at home, we had a whole new list of names and a "nothing's gonna' stop us now" attitude. We became a team, and one way or another we were going to succeed. Robert had worked too hard for too long to turn back now.

The very next month, things started to happen for us. Somebody knew somebody who knew somebody, and some people turned up who wanted success as badly as we did. Our group did enough business to advance us to the next position with our company.

After four and a half years of struggling we were finally earning money! Our income grew each month and we've never looked back.

I'm so thankful that I was there that weekend with Robert. Had he quit, it would have been the worst mistake we'd ever made. We had no way of knowing that our success was just around the corner. We would have never have seen it happen!

Now I want to share a story about how my spouse supported me at a time in my life when I so desperately needed it.

On April 21, 2000, we were on our way home from our son's baseball game when we got a call on our cell phone. It was our daughter informing us that my mom had just called—my dad was being rushed to the hospital; they thought he'd had a stroke.

Three days later, my six brothers and sisters and I were called into a private room to meet with the doctor. He had just finished talking alone with our mom. He told us what we already knew, but didn't want to face. Our daddy had gone into a coma; everything in his body had totally shut down. Machines were all that were keeping him alive, and he would never get better.

We had to make the hardest decision any of us ever had to make in our lives. This was the first time in my life I had to face losing someone so close to me.

At the time, our business was exploding and growing and we had events and meetings scheduled every day.

Thankfully, our network marketing income had grown enough that we didn't worry about money, and our team had so many great leaders, they just stepped up and handled things for us, so we could be where we needed to be—with my mom and family. Then when it came to the things that we had to be there for, Robert just handled my part for me. That allowed me all the time I needed.

I thanked God we were involved in the network marketing! With a traditional job, I would have been forced back to work almost immediately.

Instead, Robert just handled everything for me with our business.

Afterwards, just three weeks later, our daughter was graduating from high school and we had guests coming in from out of town. Our new houseboat was ready to be delivered the week after her graduation. We'd been sharing pictures of this boat with my father for almost a year. He was as excited about the boat as we were. Now I was just "there," wherever there was, going through the motions, no help to anyone.

Suddenly, my mom was in pain, and we took her to the emergency room, too. After five hours, we finally found out it was her gallbladder. Surgery was scheduled for the next day.

About six weeks later, we had an event planned for the Memorial Day weekend with over eighty leaders from our company coming. I had to plan everything and prepare food for all these people. I just did what I had to do to get through the weekend. Whatever It Takes!

Robert kept comforting me and supporting me through it all, letting me take my time to pull myself back together. I was struggling with a lot on my mind all the time.

Before I knew it, over two months had passed and I had done very little in our business. I felt like I was ready to get back to work, but I had been so out of touch that I had no clue where to start to get involved again.

It finally hit me at an event we hosted on our boat in June. We do a **Whatever It Takes!** workshop where we teach people to work on themselves more than they work on the actual business itself. We share our true-life experiences of how we turned our lives around with positive attitudes.

Robert's always telling people,

"You can't stay positive and hang around the negative."

I know he probably meant it for the whole class, but in my mind he was talking to me. I wasn't hanging around the negative; I was just *staying away from the positive*.

I wasn't reading or listening to motivational or inspirational books and tapes. I wasn't attending the events in order to hang around positive people.

I thought about it and realized that I was missing out! If I ever needed a positive attitude in my life, now was definitely the time. I knew that if I was ever going to get back to being myself and doing the things I had done before with our business, I needed to be back around positive people.

That **Whatever It Takes!** workshop got me back on track. I realized that there was nothing I could do to change anything that had happened in my life in the prior two months, but now I wanted to be happy again and be a part of our business again.

I realize now, that by reading and listening to motivational materials, and even more so, being around positive people, I can handle whatever happens in my life.

I've heard Robert teach, "The wind blows on us all; it's the set of the sail that determines the outcome."

There are always going to be difficult things happening in our lives, but as long as we can be there for each other, we can get through anything. It just takes Whatever It Takes!

Spending time on the lake with our wonderful children, Joni, and Cody.

No Time For You and Your Family?

Every tomorrow has two handles. You can take hold of the handle of anxiety or the handle of enthusiasm. Upon your choice, so will be the day.

—*Author Unknown*

I still feel like this quite often—even now after we have succeeded with network marketing and are making lots of money.

In the beginning, I blamed Robert's business as the reason he was always too busy for us, but what now? A lot of the things my husband does with his free time have nothing to do with the business. He's really into hunting: elk hunting, deer hunting, turkey hunting—you name it, he loves to hunt it.

Years ago, he dreamed of going elk hunting in Colorado. He never had the opportunity, because we simply could not afford it back then. Now that we can afford it, he goes every year and is living his dreams.

The biggest reason I still struggle with this issue is that for so long, while we struggled in the dairy business and then in network marketing, I was very dependent on Robert. I kept the house, cared for the kids and only went grocery shopping when he gave me the money. I would focus my spare time on things that:

1. Cost nothing to do.
2. Made a little money.
3. Filled my empty hours with something to do.

I had a group of friends and we met one day each week. We clipped coupons and collected box tops and wrappers for mail-in rebates. We even went to the city dump to collect the box tops and wrappers. It would take the whole day: gathering, cutting, and sorting. I did save money, and I got a few rebate checks. It was fun and rewarding for me. I even helped the local grocery store owner stock shelves and clean one day a week, so in return I could cash in my coupons on things in the store for things that I needed. All of this did help out tremendously, considering the financial situation we were in at the time.

But now I think, *Well, I can spend the whole day clipping, sorting, and gathering to save maybe one hundred dollars a month, or I can spend the whole day relaxing by the pool talking to people on the phone about our network marketing business and earn an unlimited amount of money.*

I've finally seen the big picture in network marketing and how it can change your life. I want more!

The reality has set in: we've done it. We can live our dreams.

Robert is living his dreams. He works our business whenever he wants, wherever he goes. He has people all over the country who have the same hobbies he does, and as he travels all over to help them with the business, they put him onto a hunt of a lifetime.

On the other hand, I didn't know for a long while what I wanted to do. I had a lot of material things on my list of dreams, most of which I now have. But what did I *really* want to do?

One thing I did a few years ago was to learn to play golf. First, of course, with Robert, and for a long time I would not go unless he could go too. But we finally had some friends join us in learning the game, and I found I could go with them and still have fun. This gave me some more confidence in myself to do something that I liked without my spouse. It gave me feeling of independence as well.

I have always liked spending a lot of time with our kids. We would go shopping and out to dinner. We'd ride go-carts or play miniature golf. But I realized they were growing up and had their own friends to do things with, so I found myself again wondering, *What is it I want?*

I thank God for the people in our business who really want to succeed, because through them I discovered that I love to help people.

I love to see others succeed and get the things in life that they deserve. It's kind of like seeing your kids grow up and do a good job in school.

Robert and I can afford to travel with our business, so we spend more time together now than we ever have. I love to travel! That was something that was unheard of in the dairy business. In the summertime, we take our kids and we all get to see new places together.

Our lives have changed so much over the years, and network marketing has given us the personal growth and the income to make changes in our lives.

I thoroughly enjoy spending time at the lake on our house-boat. Robert got us a neat little ski boat and I love going over to the property we bought up there and just floating out in the lake on the ski boat and looking up at our mountain.

I don't struggle too much anymore with what to do. I just do anything I want to do! I can sleep in late, I can lie out by the pool, talk on the phone, go shopping—you name it, I can do it. I don't wake up to an alarm clock reminding me it's time to go to work. Each day I think, Wow! Sometimes I have to pinch myself to see if this is really real.

I am so glad that I got involved with my spouse and network marketing. It is truly an awesome lifestyle!

And I'm doing what I love. I'm helping people do Whatever It Takes everyday!

Aerial view of our 1,000 acres on the lake.

24/7 Home Office

Yesterday is a cancelled check; tomorrow is a promissory note; today is the only cash you have, so spend it wisely.

—Kay Lyons

Since my husband and I have owned our own business most of our lives, I've learned to deal with the business twenty-four hours a day.

The thing that I like the most about working from my own home is being able to pick and choose my own hours and work around my kids and family schedules. I can be home when my kids arrive home from school. If they need me for anything, I can be at their school in less than five minutes.

I have a separate room in our house for my office. Network marketing requires some phone work, so I can talk on the phone wherever I am in the house or outside by the pool with a portable phone, or at the lake with a cell phone. I like the idea of working my business wherever I am. I also like the fact that I can dress casually and comfortably for work.

Working from home and choosing your own hours allows you the opportunity to sleep in if you want and take a break when you like.

Remember though, with network marketing, you are your own boss, and you generally get paid what you are worth; you do have to employ yourself.

It's really easy to take a break in front of the television, get interested in a movie, and suddenly your "break" has lasted for two or three hours, so be careful. It's also easy to get tied up in housework or yard work and forget you have a business to run!

Probably the toughest adjustment occurs when you and/or your spouse take that step to go full time in network marketing. At this point you've been accustomed to going to work every day and then all of a sudden you don't have to answer to anyone but yourself. You tell yourself, *I'll make those calls later,* and it feels good to sleep in for a change. You're also used to just one of you or both of you being out of the house all day; you've had a routine and now it's all out of whack.

This causes tension with many couples. One or the other messes up the house and doesn't clean it up. There are sometimes arguments over who did what and what was accomplished that day with the network marketing business. Sometimes priorities get a little out of order. What one person feels is important for the business may be totally opposite from what their spouse feels is important.

Before making the decision to go full-time, sit down with your spouse and make a plan together.

First, be sure you are financially ready. A lot of people struggle in the beginning. From my own experiences, struggling is not fun. You and your spouse should decide together what your expectations are.

There may be parts of the network marketing business that one of you can easily handle or wants to handle. If you are working a job and your spouse will be working from home, let him or her know up front what you want to come home to. If you are used to coming home from work to a neat, clean house, you won't be very happy if you walk in and the place is a mess and your spouse is taking a nap. Get all those details worked out and agreed on in advance. This way there won't be any unwanted and unhappy surprises.

When we decided to go full-time in network marketing, I was already a stay-at-home mom. Basically, my duties were to take care of our kids, cook, clean the house, do laundry and take messages. In the summer, I also took care of the outside chores, like mowing the grass. I also handled the paperwork and the bookkeeping for our business.

After I had gone through the worst of my struggles and learned more about our business, I became very excited about our opportunity.

But I was still very scared to talk to anyone. I was so excited that Robert was willing to do that part of the business for us; I would gladly do everything else.

As time passed and we were still struggling financially, the fights were on. I felt like I was keeping up my end of the deal and he wasn't. After all, my jobs were behind the scenes and never ending. I learned that talking to people is what makes you money in network marketing and since we weren't making money, I blamed him. I felt he wasn't doing his job.

There were days when Robert didn't have any appointments or he didn't make any calls. Instead, he would lie on the couch and watch television, or take off and go fishing. I would get so angry, because regardless, I always had plenty to do. Our happy decision to go full-time with network marketing was turning into an unhappy one; I was resentful in a big way.

Fortunately for us, things did get better. I had discovered the importance of believing in myself. Our love for each other gave us the strength to hold on through the tough times. Yours will too, as long as you are open and honest with each other. Talk with each other. Make plans for the business together.

Whether you work the business with your spouse or not, be a team player. If you sit down together, set your goals, create a game plan, and know what is going on, you won't be surprised when it is Tuesday night and your spouse has a meeting to attend and you are the one keeping the home fires burning.

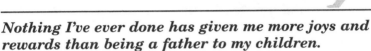

Kids and Network Marketing

Nothing I've ever done has given me more joys and rewards than being a father to my children.

—*Bill Cosby*

For anyone who has children, trying to juggle family and career can be tough! When I started working our network marketing business with my husband, I started running into unexpected difficulties when it came to my kids.

I had always been able to attend special dinners at school and go on field trips with my kids. I'd always been there for them for just about everything they'd done.

Now that I'm traveling more with my spouse and participating full-time with our business, I'm faced with decisions between kids and career. The older our kids get, the more activities they become involved in and the more I find myself having to choose between business events and kid's events.

I am now as involved in our business as Robert is. I am now one of the company's trainers and leaders. I now have responsibilities with our business, and there are events I can't possibly miss.

When I first started doing this, I was so

excited to finally be a part of something. I could finally be me! I had come so far! But when business events started run-ning into my kids' schedules, I started feeling guilty.

I had finally found my purpose in life. I had overcome so much and I was so happy that I was helping others. I had finally become my own person. People knew me as *me*, not just Robert's wife, or Joni and Cody's mom. I was making a difference in other people's lives. People were coming to me for advice with their business—my self-esteem soared.

This all started during the summer, while my kids were out of school, so they traveled with us a lot. Then, when school started again, their lives got really busy. They both are very active in clubs, organizations, and sports. I was faced with practices, games, and our business events; I felt torn apart... right down the middle.

I sat down with the kids' schedules and my events, and updated my day planner. Then I got the kids together, and we discussed the importance of each event. We came up with a plan and a schedule where everyone was happy.

There would always be that last-minute event that I didn't have written down that would conflict, but we would work it out.

Sometimes I have to look at my business as my job. With a real job, I know I would miss out on a lot more. Most days I am able to be at home when my kids come home from school. During holidays and summer break, we have a lot of time to do things together.

The flexibility of scheduling with network marketing has allowed me to be there for my kids. The personal growth that I've gained has made a huge impact on them. They've seen the changes in me; they hear and see my positive attitude on a daily basis. They have learned how to set goals and achieve them. I feel like all the changes I have gone through have had a positive impact on my whole family.

I know which events are the most important for my kids and I never miss one. I feel very fortunate that the corporate leaders of our company believe that family comes first, and they always understand when I have to miss a business event to be with my children. My kids also understand how important certain business events are for me and they support me.

I've only had one time when I had to make a major choice. Robert and I were to be promoted to the top position with our company, and on the same weekend, Cody was having his first part in a school play, a special school dinner, and his first judo competition. There will always be another event where I can be recognized, but there will never be another first play or a first judo competition for Cody. It really wasn't even a decision at all; my priority was Cody.

Another thing we do with our kids that really helps them to understand why we do the things we do is that we all sit down—Mom, Dad, and kids—and set our goals.

We ask each other, "What do we want from our business?" We plan vacations, things for the house, and fun things to do with the kids. We explain to them what we have to do in order to reach these goals, and then they understand completely when we have to miss a game or a practice.

We also make a dream board where we have pictures of the things we want and goal cards with our goals written down where we can see it every day. This really helps when the kids ask, "Why is daddy or mommy always on the phone or gone to a meeting?" We can just look at our dream board with the kids and remind them why. Our dream board also keeps us motivated and focused on our business. We have our kids add some of their own dreams and goals as well. It gets pretty exciting around our house when someone gets to mark "achieved" on that goal!

I believe all the motivational materials our kids have been exposed to because of our business have made a difference for all of us.

Some people see network marketing as a negative when it comes to kids. I hear things like, "I can't go because I have the kids." In those cases, I just move on to the next person, because I know if I had a *real job* and a *real boss*, I would be missing a lot of my kids' lives. At least I know I have a choice.

Network marketing has been the best thing ever for my family and me. Nothing we've done in the past would ever have allowed us the quality time that we now have with our kids. Spending summers at the lake and the trips we've taken together as a family while working our business are full of wonderful memories that will stay with us forever.

I want to share just a few of those special moments we've had together.

Each year—before we started making money—I would just get out the J.C. Penney's catalog and select what I felt was absolutely necessary when it came time to buy school clothes. I did this because I knew what we could and couldn't afford and I could pay it off in monthly installments. I didn't want to say again, "Honey, we can't afford that." Once the order came in, the kids were surprised and happy because they had something new. For years, my kids told their friends all their new clothes came from UPS.

One day a couple of years ago, I decided to take the kids shopping for school clothes. After all, now we could afford whatever they selected. We made a whole day of it—what a great day it was!

We went from one store to the next, shopping and buying, buying and shopping. We had just left the shoe store where both kids selected two pair of shoes each, and we had carried them to the car so our hands were free to carry things from the next store.

As we started back to the mall—all three of us holding hands, laughing and talking—Cody just stopped. He knew this store carried one particular brand of jeans that he really, really wanted. But he knew they were expensive, and he looked up at me as if he knew the answer was no and said, "Mom, can we go in here and get some of those jeans?"

I had a flashback to the times when I used to have to say, "We would if we could," and realized we could now. So I said, "You bet we can!" He just stared and said,

"Mom, I'm so glad you and Dad found that network marketing business so we can now afford this stuff!"

I know we don't want to spoil our kids totally rotten—spoiling them ripe maybe—but I must admit it sure felt good to be able to do that and know that I could afford it.

Our daughter Joni's senior prom was coming up in three months. We had had some bad weather and the schools were closed for the day, because a lot of our back roads were still covered with snow. We were sitting around deciding what to do. Somehow the suggestion came up that we just load up and go shopping in Little Rock.

Joni had wanted a pink prom dress for three years, and every year we didn't shop early enough to find one that she liked. But this year we had plenty of time, so off we went for a day of shopping and found the perfect one. We could literally afford any dress in the store; I didn't even look at the price tag, I just wrote the check. I was so excited that we were in a position financially to be able to do that for our daughter on such a special occasion.

One day during spring of that same year, our son came home from school with a brochure on Michael Jordan's basketball camp in Chicago. I didn't even know there was such a thing—we live in Faulkner County, in the middle of Arkansas. Cody started begging to go. I knew how busy we already were with our business, and the company was planning a big event around the same time. We were expected to attend, but the exact date and location had not been announced.

As it turned out, our event was the same weekend and it was in Chicago. *Wow!*

Yes, Cody attended Michael Jordan's basketball camp and had an awesome time!

Now I want to share a couple of stories about our parents and our dream board.

Each year, we write and post our goals and dreams.

We don't always know how these will get achieved, but we do know they will never be achieved if we don't write them down.

What happens is that we see our goals and dreams every day and our subconscious mind goes to work on ways to achieve them.

At the beginning of 1999, we set a goal to get my mom a new car by the end of the year. Her car was eight years old, had a lot of miles, and was beginning to have problems. We didn't buy the car for her, because...

Her boss gave her one for Christmas!

I found this out early in December, so I went to work on something else for her. In the company we're with, I can save a lot of money on jewelry, so I suggested to Daddy that he buy her a ring, and I told him I would get it for him to give to her. I knew she wanted it badly; in fact, she had already picked it out and had planned on eventually getting it for herself. I had to tell her little white lies, like they didn't have it in stock, but I would keep looking and maybe she'd have it by Christmas.

On Christmas day we always let the kids and grandkids open gifts first, and Mom and Daddy have to wait, so we can all see what they get when they open their presents. We set the stage with the song, "Still the One," as my mom opened this present from my dad.

It was the most beautiful moment and the best Christmas ever! We had no way of knowing that this would be the last Christmas together with my dad. But God knew and made things happen the way they did so that our family could have that special memory.

It's not about what we can or cannot afford or how much money we make or don't make. It's about being in the right place at the right time and making a difference in other people's lives.

My dad was not the type of person to openly show his emotions and his love, even though he mellowed as he got older. He also didn't believe in spending much money on gifts; he usually gave me a much smaller budget to work with. I'm so thankful that he agreed with my plan that year. The memories of that Christmas are so special to my whole family... especially for my mom.

Another goal we had posted on our board was to find a new house for my mother-in-law. One of Robert's three sisters was very active with us in the business, and we discussed this a lot. She called me one day in late November, after returning from a day of shopping with her other two sisters. She said, "You won't believe it, we're buying Mom a house for Christmas!"

It turned out that the other two sisters had the same dream we did. So the four of them went shopping and handed my mother-in-law the keys to her brand-new house on Christmas Eve 1999.

Network marketing has not just changed our income—it has changed our lives in many ways. We have been able to see so many dreams come true for so many people. It's just a good feeling when you know that something you did or said made a difference for somebody else.

Our dreams and goals get bigger every day, and we know, because of what we've learned from this business, that we will reach them.

Leave Me Out of It! I'm Happy Where I'm At... I Don't Want Any Part of Network Marketing!

You can't help someone get up a hill with out getting closer to the top yourself.

—Gen. H. Norman Schwarzkopf

I hear this a lot. It's OK if you want to continue on in the career you have chosen. No one expects you to quit what you are doing to follow your spouse's dreams. You are your own person, and you have your own vision and goals in life. I would have never become supportive and gotten involved just for my spouse. I had to figure out what I wanted.

As I've already shared, in the beginning I was down and out, financially and emotionally. Network marketing was a big negative in my life. I probably would have been better off if I had a job or a career, because it would have given me something to do besides worry.

As time went by and things started happening with my spouse's business and he was succeeding, he often tried to involve me in his business but I rejected all his attempts. I had what network marketers call the "I.T.C. syndrome"; better known as the "I'm Too Cool syndrome."

I had listened to so many people make fun of what my spouse was doing that I

was totally ignoring his success.

I believed them instead of him.

I heard things like: "He's a born salesman. He can do that, but we can't. When is he going to get a real job? When is he going to wake up from his dream world and come back to reality with us? That kind of success doesn't happen in the real world."

Since I didn't have a clue as to what network marketing was all about, I didn't have any comeback for the things I was hearing.

I found myself wanting to believe, but I wouldn't let myself. After all, someone had to be logical and responsible; we did have a family to think about. I couldn't let myself exist in his dream world—we couldn't live our future on dreams! I even checked the want ads on a regular basis for some kind of a job, just in case. To me, having a job meant security for our future.

I had living proof that the products we were marketing worked, and proof that the pay structure worked; we were receiving checks and they never bounced. The company had been in business for several years, I knew it was here to stay; but yet, I could barely mention what Robert was doing to people and I got shot down pretty quickly whenever I did.

I was buying everyone else's stories. I was buying the traditional way of thinking: only people who get lucky succeed.

Everyone had me believing that Robert was just plain lucky. They would say, "Ever since I've known him, he could fall into a pile of cow manure and come out smelling like a rose." I had heard someone say that about Robert long before we ever saw network marketing, so I believed it. I finally came to the conclusion that the people I knew had normal lives and were happy, and I was not going to tell them they could live their dreams with this thing called network marketing. They knew and I knew that Robert's success was really just luck.

I was perfectly happy that he was so lucky. After all, our bills were now being paid and I didn't have to worry anymore. I began to realize that his dreams were coming true, luck or no luck; there was definitely something real here.

I got more involved to see what this network marketing thing was all about, to see if it could possibly help me to have some of the things in my dreams, too.

I started attending events and learning the business. Nothing was forced on me; I participated at my own pace. I got to know the people involved, from the corporate level to the leaders in the field to the brand-new distributors. One thing I realized is that they were all normal people just like me. I realized they all had dreams and goals and a lot of them were not only going for them, they were achieving them with network marketing. It wasn't just Robert being lucky.

Talk about rags-to-riches stories—I heard a lot of them! I also met a lot of professionals—doctors, lawyers, and business owners—who had actually changed careers to do their network marketing business full-time.

I was amazed at the success stories of people from all walks of life. There were high school dropouts to college graduates to millionaires getting involved.

And what was so wonderful and strange, was that everyone

had the same opportunity to succeed regardless of their background.

Even though I had heard my whole life how important a college education was, so you could get a higher paying job, I planned to get married and go into the dairy farming business when I graduated from high school. I even turned down two basketball scholarships because I didn't think I needed a degree for dairy farming, so I never went to college.

After all our struggles in the dairy business and then in network marketing, I still believed that something better and something real would come along. I had already lost out on a college degree, but something was out there.

While still hoping and searching, I continued to support Robert by attending events. I began to realize, *This thing is real! These people are real people!* The more I was around network marketing, the more I liked it and the more I believed in it. I was now surrounding myself with positive people and not getting bogged down with the negatives.

I began thinking, *What if we can succeed?* What used to be Robert's dream world was now becoming *our* dream world.

I liked what was happening.

There were a lot of changes taking place in our lives. We were now doing things we had only dreamed of before. I was reading books and listening to motivational tapes constantly. I had a better attitude towards life. Our kids were happy, we were happy, and I no longer cared if other people laughed at us. I knew there were plenty of other people out there just like us, and our job was to find them and to help them realize their dreams.

I look back at where we were when we started and where we are now, and I know that network marketing has changed our lives. I try not to brag; I don't want to come across as conceited, because I'm not. But our monthly checks total more than a lot of college-degreed jobs pay in a year. I've learned that I can't dwell on the ones who don't see or want network marketing. I focus on the ones who do and help them to succeed.

I'm not asking you as a spouse to forget your dreams and goals.

Just open your mind so you too can learn to be as supportive as possible. It just might be the encouragement your spouse needs to succeed.

I know lots of people who are succeeding with network marketing who tell me their spouses don't want any part of the business, but he or she supports them in what they are doing. They have taken the time to share with their spouses what they're doing, how they're doing it, and why. They have explained their business, shown a video, or have taken their spouses to an event. They have given their spouses the opportunity to hear from others in their business.

They have also set goals together. They have shared with their spouse their plan of action: what, when, and where they are and where they are going with their business. By doing this, there are no surprises and negatives. They then continue to communicate with their spouse on their progress.

It's no different than sitting down to dinner and discussing each other's day at work.

I've learned to ask questions and to be open with my

feelings. If I feel my spouse is spending too much time with a certain group of people and nothing is happening with the business, I simply ask him what is going on, and why that part of our business is not growing. I suggest that from what I've seen and heard in network marketing, it may be time to move on and say, "Next."

Sometimes we get so caught up in wanting success more for someone than that person wants it for themselves, and we fail to see that we are the only ones working.

Whether we're a partner in the business with our spouse or not, it helps to know how the business works, so we can give our spouses the encouragement they need when they need it.

All network marketing companies offer a product. If we have thoroughly researched the program and feel the product has value—why not use it? This is another way we can be supportive without actually working the business.

Most companies have conference calls, fax on demand, Internet sites, and literature that provides information about the products, the company, the pay plans, and the corporate events. By taking a little time to study this information, you can learn a lot about your spouse's business.

Just knowing that you care enough to learn what it's all about may be the support and encouragement your spouse needs.

This is a way to be supportive without being directly involved in the business. And you'll at least be able to answer a question when someone calls, which is a big help.

I was very negative in the beginning, because I didn't understand what the business was all about. I didn't want to listen to the details and the process; I just wanted to know when I was going to have the answers to my problems. I had a "forget the details, just show me the money, honey" attitude.

After I started listening to motivational tapes and reading inspirational books—which again had nothing to do with directly working the business—I began to understand why Robert persisted with his dreams and goals. I became more open-minded to the fact that this was what he had chosen to use as his vehicle to reach his dreams. He had already proven to me that my negative attitude was not going to stop him.

Now, I'm not suggesting that those working a network marketing business have no regard for their spouse's opinion.

Nor am I suggesting that your network marketing spouse is right and you are wrong. I am saying that together you can reach a happy medium.

I've also seen some marriages in network marketing turn sour. The network marketing business is often blamed, but I think that is just an excuse for a way out of taking responsibility.

However in most cases, success in network marketing requires support and communication from both spouses. If you're the one working the business, then treat it like a business and not a hobby. Be serious when you set your goals and make it happen. Spend your time wisely and effectively.

It's much easier for a negative spouse to take a second look if they can see some progress.

When I started understanding what Robert's business was about, even though I wasn't out in the field with him, I learned little ways of helping out.

Rather than just take a message, I was able to answer questions from new people in our business. This gave Robert more time to work his business and be with our family, rather than spend that time returning phone calls.

I learned how to fill out applications, place orders, and read reports. I knew when and where the events were so I could also pass that on when people called. I started handling the behind-the-scenes stuff, so he could have more time to talk to people.

I did everything from my home, at my convenience, around my schedule. This gave me something to do with my spare time, plus it made me feel needed and useful to our business. It made me feel a part of something and good about myself again.

You may love what you're doing now and not want to be part of your spouse's business.

But I encourage you to allow your spouse to share with you what their business is all about.

Get all your questions answered.

See what it is that has them so excited.

This way you'll know what's going on and what you're up against. You will run into conflicts, but knowing what your spouse's business is really about will help you better understand and hopefully your conflicts will be discussions instead of arguments.

After you've learned all about your spouse's business, let your spouse know your feelings. For or against, let them know where you stand with their business.

You're a team in marriage and a team for life. Whatever It Takes!, keep it that way. Always be open and honest with your feelings and together you will survive and thrive.

Another hard day at work on our Cobalt ski boat we named, Pocket Change.

Having fun on the lake.

I Want to Do It Too!

Dream it! See it! Believe it! Achieve it!
You miss 100 percent of the shots you never take!

—*Wayne Gretzky*

Robert had already become successful and was earning a lot of money when I decided I wanted to do what he was doing. I was already a partner with him in the business—a silent partner. Like I said earlier, people always said, "Oh, so you're Robert's wife."

I was really working hard; our business had grown. I was doing all of the "manual" work. Besides my responsibilities as a mother, a wife, the maid, the laundry lady, and the kid's taxi, I was handling all the paperwork, bookkeeping, and scheduling events. At the events I did all the decorating. I loaded and unloaded products, set up the displays, and ran the registration table.

It finally hit me one day, I was doing all the hard stuff and all Robert was doing was showing up, shaking hands, and talking to people.

Robert always seemed so relaxed, just visiting and meeting

new people. I was always stressing and running around like a chicken with my head cut off making sure everything was done.

I had become a true believer in our products, and after meeting the corporate leaders, I believed in the company. I believed in myself. But I felt like everyone expected me to be as good in front of the room as Robert was, because I had been there the whole time he had been involved with network marketing.

I was always in his life, but not always in his business. By this time, I knew just as much about the business as he did, but I had never shared my knowledge in front of a group.

I watched Robert go through stage fright in the beginning, and he persisted until he was totally comfortable and relaxed as if he had done that his whole life. I knew, too, that I would have to stumble through until I was comfortable. Again, one major problem:

I was scared to death of public speaking.

I remember one of our events where Robert had been on stage all day and had almost lost his voice completely. As we were driving home he caught me feeling sorry for him in a weak moment. So, he had asked me to help him the next month. I figured there wouldn't be very many people there— *after all,* I thought, *the group can't grow that much in 30 days,* so I agreed to do one 30 minute class.

I practiced and practiced; I was ready for my class. But I wasn't ready for a room full of over 125 people!

I panicked. I begged. I pleaded. I tried everything to get Robert to let me out of having to do that class. All he would say was, "Do the thing you fear the most, and the death of fear is certain."

I did the class, and afterwards I felt so good, I felt like I could do anything. I finally made up my mind that I could do it, and I managed to stumble and stutter through a couple of small speaking parts for our company.

Every time a new product was released, I'd think, Here's my chance! Then I would chicken out.

After every big event or training, I would get all motivated and tell myself again, *Here's my chance,* only to chicken out again.

Remember, what sells in network marketing are stories. Sure the products, the compensation plan, and the company all have to be good, but stories are what sell.

The old saying goes, "Facts tell, but stories sell."

We always teach people to develop their story. What makes a new person join are the stories they hear, stories they can relate to; it may be someone with the same background or someone they know. It's someone's story that helps them to see themselves doing this. I would attend the events and hear those stories and get excited all over again... only to go home and chicken out about telling my own.

What finally made me realize that I had to do it—that no matter how scared I was, I had to get up and speak—was the people.

At the events, our one-on-one conversations during the breaks showed me that others had the same fears I had. These conversations were very inspiring!

I knew everything about our business. I could answer any questions that anyone had. I found that the one thing we had in common was the fear of public speaking. I knew if I could overcome that fear, so could a lot of others. My doing so would not only change my life, but would change the lives of others as well.

My desire to make a difference for others became so strong, I would not let myself chicken out any longer. I accepted the fact that I would not be all that great the first time up, but I would learn from my mistakes. The main thing was *to do it.*

And you know, each time it got easier. People now tell me how they can relate to what I say; they tell I helped them or inspired them to move on with their business. If they only knew what they had done for me!

Knowing that I've made a difference in other people's lives has been the most wonderful reward of all. It's been worth whatever nervousness I've had to go through.

Since I have begun to work every aspect of the business with Robert, I have learned something. Our business is growing twice as fast and we are able to help twice as many people! What a concept! **Whatever It Takes!** I love it!

Having Fun!

You're only going to live life once, enjoy it while you can!

—Joe Lasley, my daddy

I never dreamed that I could have so much fun and get paid for it!

As I told you earlier, network marketing is basically people helping people. Robert and I and our kids have had the opportunity to travel and meet a lot of really great people. We've been able to see a lot of wonderful places, and stay at a lot of beautiful resorts and hotels—and talk about fine dining, *wow!*

For instance, we took our kids to Chicago to attend a big event, traveling with another couple. They were friends of ours who had joined us in our network marketing company. We all had a few extra days to stay and see the town. So, we toured the John Hancock building, and after that... wow, was I surprised!

Did you know Chicago has a beach? Before that trip, I thought all the beaches were in Florida.

We walked Navy Pier, taking in the rides, restaurants, and fun. We ate pizza at the most famous—and the first—pizza restaurant in Chicago called Uno's Pizza. You don't find pizza like that in Arkansas! This was a very educational and exciting trip for the whole family.

Robert and I went to Orlando, Florida, for a convention and our hotel had a restaurant that served the meal they did on the *Titanic*. They had an original menu and put together a dinner just like it. It was wonderful! I can't say that I've ever had the salad *after* the main entrée before—once again, a totally new experience for me.

We've had the opportunity to share so many things with our kids because of our network marketing business. They've had the opportunity to meet kids from other states, and develop friendships they would have never known otherwise.

There are occasions when we don't have time to explore the event city, but the kids still have a blast. They go swimming, watch television, and order room service. To our family, staying in a hotel is a vacation. We don't have to cook and wash dishes, we don't have to make our beds or clean our room. We all really like that!

Together as a family, we've played in the ocean several times, been up in the Arch in St. Louis, and attended a Cardinal's game when Mark McGuire hit two of his record home run hits. We've been to Six Flags in Texas and St. Louis. We've been to Disney World, taken a rides in limos, gone on a boat ride in Lake Michigan, and deep-sea fishing in the ocean. We've traveled to Branson, Missouri several times. We've been able to do so much with our kids! And Robert and I get a lot of weekend getaways together as well.

Everywhere we go, we work our business and meet new people; it's a pretty awesome lifestyle!

We really enjoy the travel; after all, we're two ex-broke dairy farmers who never had the opportunity to leave the farm unless we could get back before the evening milking.

We've been on five Caribbean cruises as rewards from our company, but most of our travels have been within the United States, because that is where our business is.

And talk about dreams coming true:

One day, when Robert made me sit down and write down our dreams and goals, I wrote that I wanted to go on a trip to Europe. Robert said that just wasn't his cup of tea, but if I really wanted it... write it down anyway. After all what we were doing was dreaming.

I figured that if Robert wanted it we would get it. If not, we wouldn't. I still wrote it down and put it on my dream board. I saw that every day for eight years.

One day our son Cody came home from school with brochures from Europe. He said one of the teachers was putting together a trip and if enough people wanted to go she could make it happen. Guess what? In the spring of 2005, eight women and seven teenage boys—including me and Cody—spent ten glorious days touring France and Italy! It truly was a dream come true!

Three years ago we cut out a great picture from a *Robb Report* magazine of a hacienda in Puerto Vallarta called Casa Demae, and added that to our dream board. On Labor Day of 2005, Robert and I, along with five other couples, spent five nights and six beautiful days in that very villa!

It was one of the most luxurious and relaxing vacations we

had ever taken or ever even imagined. There were thirteen people waiting on us hand and foot. Lying in the sun by the infinity pool, they wouldn't let us get up to grab a bottle of water ourselves. They even washed and ironed our underwear—and *gift-wrapped* them—pink ribbon for girls, blue for boys. We were treated like kings and queens.

Not only could we afford all of it because of our network marketing business, all the other couples we went with are in our business as well and they're making money, too.

As we travel, all the beautiful places to see and all the fun things to do amaze me. Sometimes people ask us if travel is required to work this business. We travel because we want to. At times, we probably relax more while traveling than we do at home. It's not a requirement, but it does help in building your business, especially if you want your business to expand into other states or countries.

We met a couple through our business that have become dear friends. They live in a beautiful log home on a mountaintop near Eureka Springs, Arkansas. We sometimes go stay with them for a few days at a time so the guys can hunt, the girls can shop, and in between we work our business together over the phone. Talk about relaxing! The view from their home is absolutely gorgeous!

We met another couple from Florida who took us to the most beautiful park, located on the Rainbow River near their home. That river is crystal clear; we even went on a float trip while we were there. We went with a whole group of people in our business and had a blast!

We worked with another couple from Louisiana for a couple

of days. We had a company event for two nights, and our days were free. The guys went fishing and the wife took me for a tour of the town. This is where I ate my first meat pie and dirty rice; it was different, but good. The town was an old historic one with brick streets alongside a river. It was really interesting!

We spent another weekend with some people in Oklahoma, and I stayed in my first bed-and-breakfast. It was a very old historic house filled with antiques. It's funny how these sorts of things "wow" us as we get older. While growing up in school, you sometimes think history is useless and can't wait for the bell to ring.

I could go on for hours with stories like this. My point is, working our business is always fun, new and exciting. It doesn't even feel like work anymore.

We usually try to schedule our travels so we can spend time away from the event with the people.

We like to get to know the folks in our business, to find out what it is they want from it, and learn how we can help.

We like to get to know them better so they feel more comfortable with us helping them. We may have a barbecue before a meeting, or go to someone's house after a meeting, just to relax and visit.

We find one thing in common everywhere we go. We find real people... people who have dreams and goals and who want more from life.

I didn't know that I could feel at home in so many places. We have met some of the best people through network marketing. The friendships we have built are the greatest! The hospitality we have been shown is second to none!

For people who can't or don't want to travel, this type of business can be worked from your home: over the phone, through the Internet, direct mail, etc. Check out your options with your company. I spend a lot of time in my summer office, which is a swimming pool in my yard or on our houseboat at the lake. I relax, get a tan, talk on the phone, and make money! *Wow!*

Five years ago, we spent two days in Somerset, Kentucky, picking out and custom designing our new 18' x 80' Somerset houseboat. We designed the whole thing ourselves from the floor plans to the flooring, furniture, colors, even the fabrics for the window covers and beds. We decided on four bedrooms and two baths with a large living room and kitchen area. The rooftop deck has a fly-bridge where we can operate the boat from the top deck as well as from the helm. We put a rooftop cover at the front of the upper deck with the back open for sun tanning. We added a slide off the back for the kids.

We took delivery of that new boat in May 2000, and wow, have we had a blast with it! We regularly take people out for a sunset cruise while showing them our business. We've carried groups of as many as 130 people. We have had several training events on the boat as well.

We designed a workshop for people in our business where they can come to Arkansas, spend some time on our boat, and learn how to build a big business. We call it the **"Whatever It Takes!"** workshop.

A local restaurant supplies meals and meeting space, and the local hotels accommodate our overnight guests. We spend about an hour after dinner in the meeting room and wrap up the first night with a cruise across the lake. The next day is spent in the workshop classroom, and then it's back to the boat for fun, hamburgers, and working the phones for the business.

We try to get about five or six of these workshops in before the summer season ends. That has proven to make a positive difference in the lives of the people who have attended. I've seen many people overcome their fears during these workshops. Once we get out on the lake, I've seen people who could not swim and were afraid of the water, jump in! I've also seen people jump off of the top of the boat when they had a fear of heights. I've seen many people conquer their fear of picking up the telephone.

Once they recognize some of these fears and overcome them, they realize they can do Whatever It Takes! to succeed.

The group setting makes a difference because people realize others are overcoming their fears, too.

We leave the boat a few times during the summer to travel across the country for company events. During those summer months, our two kids usually travel with us. That's why it worked out so perfectly for Cody to go to Michael Jordan's basketball camp; we were all going to Chicago anyway!

We had become friends with a couple from Chicago who joined our business about five years ago and who have two kids close to the same age as ours. We went early to spend some time with them and work our business. They recently built their dream home, and it is absolutely beautiful! We spent the day sunning on the back deck, talking on the phone and working our business. The guys went four-wheeling, fishing, swimming, and played games. They had a blast! The girls went shopping at the mall. We had a wonderful barbeque and wrapped the evening up with an awesome business meeting with their local people.

Probably one of the biggest blessings we've had in spending time with people is the opportunity to really get to know my sister and brother-in-law. Robert's sister Rita and her husband Donnie joined us in the business seven years ago and have done quite well. I've had the opportunity to watch them grow with their dreams.

We've spent a lot of time together, not just working, but having fun as well. We've traveled all over the country together attending events and having a blast. Our relationship has become much closer than ever before. It's more like we're best friends, rather than family.

We share the same dreams and goals, and helping each other achieve them is one of the best parts of this business. It truly is awesome to see others succeed, but it really is special when it's family.

We now spend time together other than just at family reunions and special holidays. It's great!

People ask me all the time how many hours I work per week. I honestly don't know; when you're having fun, it's not work! All I know is, we just keep doing everything I've shared with you and every week we get checks in our mailbox. It doesn't get any better than that!

Afterword

Whatever your doubts or fears, I hope this book has helped. I know I haven't experienced everything, and I don't claim to have all the answers, but I have seen a lot. Remember, whatever it is you're going through, someone else is going through it too. Talk to people; they can help you!

You will probably find yourself in a lot of the situations that I've shared with you.

Understand that when you do, you will have to live it, experience it, and grow from it. You will survive it.

No one makes it to the top in network marketing without some struggles.

Your and your spouse will struggle in totally different ways.

Your spouse will have others in their business to encourage them and help them, and you will probably feel all alone.

Just remember, *you are not alone.*

If I've learned one thing from sharing my stories, it's that there are a lot of spouses in this business who have the same doubts and struggles that I have.

If your struggles are like any of mine, I hope my stories will help you get through them with a little less pain.

I love our network marketing business. It's more of a lifestyle than a job or a business. We are truly living our dreams today.

I was asked one time, if I had it all to do over again, what would I change?

I wouldn't change a thing.

I honestly believe that everything happens for a reason and if just one thing had been changed I don't think we would be where we are today. We look back at all the tough times and remember all we have learned. You learn more from your mistakes than you do from your successes. One of my lessons was finding out that network marketing is a personal growth program disguised as a business.

Whether you are actively involved with your spouse or not, it really is the opportunity of a lifetime! Find your part in your spouse's business—helping or supporting or making it your own—and start living your dreams today!

Network marketers' time has come!

Don't miss it, grab your dreams and don't let go and we'll see you on the beaches of the world!

I wish you all the happiness in the world, and may all your dreams come true, **Whatever It Takes!**

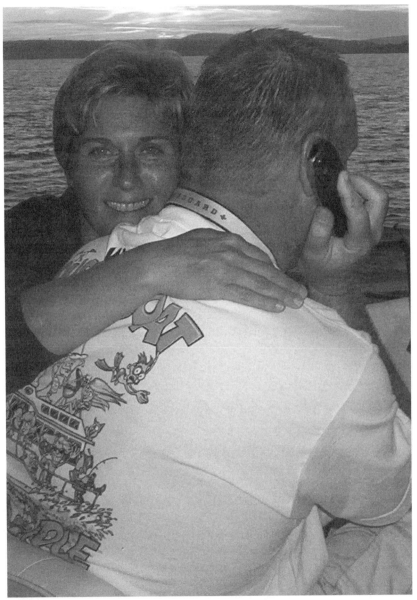

We're living our dream, we wish the same for you.